In His Name

Kirkie Morrissey

NAVPRESS ●®

A MINISTRY OF THE NAVIGATORS
P.O. Box 6000, Colorado Springs, CO 80934

The Navigators is an international Christian organization.
Jesus Christ gave His followers the Great Commission to
go and make disciples (Matthew 28:19). The aim of The
Navigators is to help fulfill that commission by multiply-
ing laborers for Christ in every nation.

NavPress is the publishing ministry of The Navigators.
NavPress publications are tools to help Christians grow.
Although publications alone cannot make disciples or
change lives, they can help believers learn biblical disci-
pleship, and apply what they learn to their lives and
ministries.

© 1984 by Kirkie Morrissey
All rights reserved, including translation
ISBN: 0-89109-056-8
10561

Third printing, 1986

Printed in the United States of America

Contents

To
the glory of God

Author

Kirkie Morrissey coordinated women's Bible studies in Colorado Springs, Colorado, for six years. She also trained women to lead those studies. She now acts as an advisor.

Kirkie carries on a ministry of writing Bible study material and speaking about the Christian life at retreats and conferences, and in churches. In addition to *In His Name,* she has also written *Designed by God, On Holy Ground, Get Growin',* and *A Woman's Workshop on Forgiveness.*

Before her marriage, Kirkie was on the staff of Young Life in Tacoma, Washington. She is a graduate of Wheaton College.

Acknowledgments

I would like to express my heart-felt appreciation to my dear friends Nancy Metz and Mary Lou Jacobs. Their love, prayer support, and partnership in serving the Lord mean so much to me! I would like to thank Nancy, too, for giving of her time, skills, and wisdom in reviewing these studies.

For my husband, Terry, I give thanks! His encouragement and love provide tremendous support in enabling me to communicate the messages that are on my heart.

My deepest thanks is to the Lord—for His desire to make Himself known and to be the God He is; for His consistent leading; for faithful revelation of the truths in His Word; and for the working of His Spirit to accomplish His purposes. To Him be all praise, honor, and glory.

Introduction

Why did you receive the name you have? Is there special significance to it?

Today a name is often selected according to how it sounds with one's last name rather than for what the name means. Other considerations are the feeling or image a certain name conveys, how common or uncommon it is, and who in the family merits a namesake.

However, in biblical times, the choice of names was very important, for they often communicated a message. Close attention was paid to the selection of a name. God Himself used names as an avenue to reveal His plan for an individual, underscore a specific quality of that person, or communicate a message. For example, when God chose Abram to be the father of our faith, He changed Abram's name to Abraham, meaning "father of a multitude," and to Abraham's wife, Sarai, He gave the name Sarah, meaning "princess." When Bathsheba gave birth to Solomon, the Lord gave him the name Jedidiah, meaning "loved by the Lord." The name Methuselah means basically "when he is gone it shall be sent," through which God prophesied the time of the flood. When Jesus was selecting His disciples, He changed Simon's name, which meant "shifting sand," to Cephas, or Peter, meaning "rock," which Peter truly did become.

In calling Jesus "the Word of God," the meaning is that Jesus Himself is a message from God! In Scripture where this name appears, the Greek for *word* is *logos*, which means "a word embodying a message." It's exciting to see how masterfully the Lord uses the details in everything He does. In the Bible, God's inspired written Word, the Lord God is referred to by over 400 names. Of these, more than 100 apply to Jesus Christ. Each is carefully given to communicate specific truths. Because Christ is a message from God, studying these names promises to be an adventure in discovery.

For the purpose of this study, a selection of names pertaining to Christ alone will be explored. As you study, ask the Lord to open your eyes, mind, and heart to the truths He desires to communicate in each name. In Daniel 2:47 (NASB), the Lord is referred to as the "revealer of mysteries." Ask Him to be this now for you—to reveal things of Himself you have previously not known. He *promises* to do this in Jeremiah 33:3 where He bids you "call to me and I will answer you and tell you great and unsearchable things you do not know."

Ask Him to not only *teach* you the truths about Himself through His names, but also to enable you to *experience* the truths that each name conveys! Jesus Christ desires to be to you all that each name reveals. Therefore, think of each name as a window through which you see Him more clearly and an avenue along which to experience Him more fully. As you do this, may you grow to love Him as He loves you.

1
Prince of Peace

Peace is a major issue in our world today. Individuals are seeking it as well as nations. Is it possible to have peace in our world? Is it possible for individuals to experience inner peace in the midst of difficulty, pain, or sorrow?

Jesus Christ is the Prince of Peace. This title is recorded in the same verse in which Wonderful Counselor appears, Isaiah 9:6. Jesus desires for you to experience Him as your peace. To discover how this is possible, turn to God's Word.

Your Prince of Peace

1. Read Isaiah 9:6 and Luke 2:10-14. What did the angels say would be the result of Christ's coming?

   _____

   _____

   _____

   _____

2. What does Jesus promise in John 14:27 and 16:33?

   _____

   _____

3. How would you describe the peace the world gives?

_____

_____

_____

How do you hope Jesus' peace is different?

_____

_____

_____

Initial Peace

4. Before you can experience God's peace daily, you must be reconciled to Him. Dr. Billy Graham in his book *The Holy Spirit* writes, "The peace *of* God that can reign in our hearts is always preceded by peace *with* God, which must be the starting point."[1] Why does peace with God have to be established first? Consider Romans 3:21-25 and 5:1.

_____

_____

_____

_____

5. Read Colossians 1:19-20. What did God do about man's separation from Him?

_____

_____

10

6. According to Ephesians 2:14, who is Jesus?

_____

_____

_____

7. For Him to give you peace, where must He live, as expressed in Galatians 2:20?

_____

_____

_____

8. Explain how this happens by considering the imagery of Revelation 3:20.

_____

_____

_____

_____

Have you given Christ this invitation to come into your life, bringing you peace with God? If you're not sure, would you like to? If so, write out your request to Him here, and then record His promise to you that is found in Revelation 3:20.

_____

_____

_____

_____

9. What are those things you feel anxious about? What do you think is the source of your unrest?

_____

_____

_____

_____

10. The Scriptures give insight into some causes of inner unrest.

    a. What causes are referred to in the passages below?

    Psalm 32:3-5 _____

    _____

    _____

    Luke 16:13 _____

    _____

    John 12:43 _____

    _____

    John 21:19-22 _____

    _____

    _____

    Ephesians 4:31-32 _____

    _____

b. Which of these do you struggle with?

_____

_____

_____

_____

11. Read the passage about peace in Philippians 4:6-9.

a. In what ways can your thought patterns affect God's peace?

_____

_____

_____

b. What does the Lord desire for you to do with those concerns weighing on your heart?

_____

_____

_____

_____

c. What does He promise the result will be?

_____

_____

_____

_____

d. Examine your thoughts. Are the *majority* positive thoughts, seeing the good in others and in situations, and praising the Lord for who He is and for His goodness to you?

_____

_____

_____

e. If not, confess this and ask the Lord to call it to your attention everytime you begin to dwell on the negative, and to help you replace your thoughts with His. Write your request here.

_____

_____

_____

f. What are your requests to the Lord regarding those cares, burdens, and anxieties you are experiencing? Give them to the Lord. Let Him carry them, and give you peace instead.

_____

_____

_____

_____

12. After giving each one to the Lord, what is it important for you to do, as indicated in Isaiah 26:3?

_____

_____

_____

13. What important focus will help you maintain God's peace as you apply the steps explored in this chapter?

Habakkuk 3:16-18 _____

_____

_____

Philippians 4:4 _____

_____

Hebrews 12:2 _____

_____

14. According to Revelation 21:1-4, when do you think God's peace will finally reign in its fullness, both in heaven and on earth?

_____

_____

_____

15. In conclusion, write out Paul's final greeting to the Christians in Thessalonica as found in 2 Thessalonians 3:16, reading it as his prayer for you.

_____

_____

_____

_____

_____

Questions for Further Discussion

Question 3: In what ways do people look for peace, or attempt to find peace today? How have you sought peace in the past?

Question 9: How does God discipline us? What result does He desire from His discipline in our lives according to Hebrews 12:11? How have you experienced this in the past?

Question 10: What are some other causes you have struggled with?

Question 11b: What does Peter tell you to do in 1 Peter 5:7? What reason does he give?

Question 12: Do you have difficulty trusting the Lord with your life, a particular situation, or a person you care deeply for? If so, what steps can you take to strengthen and deepen your trust?
   In his book *When God First Thought of You,* Lloyd Ogilvie writes, "Peace is volitional. We receive it only after we have surrendered our wills to do God's will at all costs."[2] How does trusting God enable you to surrender? Is there an area of your life, or a situation that you need to surrender to the Lord? Talk with Him about this now.

Question 13: Have you experienced the paradox of having the peace of Christ that surpasses understanding in the midst of deep pain, difficulty, or sorrow? Do you need this today? Pour out your heart to Him now, for He cares for you. What steps will you take next in order to keep your heart, mind, and spirit filled with His peace?

Notes
1. Billy Graham, *The Holy Spirit* (Waco, Texas: Word, Inc., 1980), page 193.
2. Lloyd J. Ogilvie, *When God First Thought of You* (Waco, Texas: Word, Inc., 1978), page 184.

2
The Good Shepherd

Throughout the Bible God refers to Himself as a shepherd. People in biblical times were very familiar with that role. Tending sheep was very common, so the truths God communicated using the imagery of a shepherd were readily understood.

Today, however, being a shepherd is not so common, but God's truths are still relevant. Therefore it's important to examine what God was communicating and apply it to our lives today.

Exploring Jesus Christ as the Good Shepherd provides an important view of His character. This is a significant place to begin. Not only is such a study important in considering who He is, it is essential if we are to allow Christ any role in our lives!

Let's begin by turning to God's Word.

The Imagery of a Shepherd

1. How would you describe a shepherd's role with his sheep? On what are you basing your understanding?

   _____

   _____

   _____

   _____

   _____

How would you describe a shepherd of people?

_____

_____

_____

_____

2. Read Isaiah 40:11. How does the Lord as a shepherd care for His flock?

_____

_____

_____

_____

How does it help you to picture yourself as one of His sheep?

_____

_____

_____

_____

Jesus as Our Shepherd

3. Read John 10:11, 14, and 15.

   a. What more is revealed here of Jesus' character as the Good Shepherd?

   _____

_____

_____

_____

b. How does this compare to the way people usually view God?

_____

_____

_____

_____

4. If you were to describe Jesus as a shepherd, what words would you use?

_____

_____

_____

_____

5. Read John 10:1-18 and 27-28.

a. According to verses 3 and 4, what does Jesus do for His sheep?

_____

_____

_____

_____

b. How would you like Him to do this for you today? Ask Him now to do so.

_____

_____

_____

_____

_____

c. In verse 9, what is conveyed to you through the imagery that in Him you will "find pasture"?

_____

_____

_____

_____

d. What is the reason Jesus says He has come? Reread verse 10.

_____

_____

_____

What quality of life does He desire to give *you?*

_____

_____

_____

e. How intimately does Jesus know His sheep? See verses 14 and 15. Consider Psalm 139:1-4 also.

_____

_____

_____

The Lost Sheep

6. Read the parable in Luke 15:3-7.

   a. What is the shepherd's attitude toward a sheep that is lost?

   _____

   _____

   _____

   b. In what ways can you, as a sheep, be lost?

   _____

   _____

   _____

   _____

   c. Do you sometimes not want Christ, the Good Shepherd, to find you? How can this passage change your attitude?

   _____

   _____

   _____

The Twenty-third Psalm

7. Read this famous psalm of David's (who himself had been a shepherd). He uses the Hebrew word *Yahweh* for Lord, increasing our understanding of the Lord as our Shepherd. Yahweh means "the God of grace; the God who is dependable; the faithful One; the God who is constant and in whom there is no change; the One who can be counted on to be all He claims to be"!

   a. What quality of His in this definition is especially meaningful to you, and why?

   _____

   _____

   _____

   _____

   b. Based upon this psalm, what can the Lord as your Shepherd do for you?

   _____

   _____

   _____

   _____

   c. What do you think is yours to do?

   _____

   _____

   _____

8. As a shepherd, Jesus uses a rod and staff, which are a source of comfort to sheep. Henry Gariepy, in *Portraits of Christ*, writes that "the rod was a stout piece of wood with which the shepherd fought off the enemies of the sheep. . . . The staff was a long, crooked stick which the shepherd would gently lay on the back of the sheep to keep it from straying and getting lost."[1]

Can you give an example of a time in which the Lord used his rod or staff to shepherd you?

_____

_____

_____

_____

9. How is Christ shepherding you today?

_____

_____

_____

_____

10. In what other ways would you like Him to shepherd you in your needs today?

_____

_____

_____

_____

Ask Jesus specifically to be your Shepherd in all the ways He desires to be.

23

Questions for Further Discussion

The questions at the conclusion of each lesson can be used for further thought and study if you are doing *In His Name* by yourself. If you are in a group, these questions can be incorporated by your leader in guiding the discussion for fuller understanding and application of the truths studied during the week.

In this lesson, discussion questions have been included for questions 1, 3, 4, 5d, and 5e. After you have discussed question 1 in the lesson itself, you can discuss the related questions below.

Question 1: In general, do people today feel the need for a shepherd? What resistance might people have to a shepherd? At what times might they appreciate having one? How do you personally feel?

Question 3: What influences helped to form your concept of God?

Question 4: Is there an authority that you can believe, where truth can be found regarding the nature of God? Consider John 17:17 and 2 Timothy 3:15-17. Can God lie? See Numbers 23:19 and Titus 1:2. What does this mean concerning what you discover about Him through His Word?

Question 5d: What is your response to this discovery?

Question 5e: What does God's intimate knowledge of you mean for you today?

Note
1. Henry Gariepy, *Portraits of Christ* (Old Tappan, New Jersey: Fleming H. Revell Company, 1974), page 65.

3
Wonderful Counselor

Approximately 745 years before Jesus Christ was born, the prophet Isaiah foretold the Savior's coming. In Isaiah 9:6 the prophet gives some names by which this Son was to be known. The first one Isaiah mentions is Wonderful Counselor. In some versions of the Bible these words have been separated by a comma, indicating two separate names. However, recent study indicates that the word *wonderful* is an adjective describing this Counselor of ours! To discover how truly wonderful He is, turn now to the Bible, God's written Word revealing Himself.

Jesus Christ's Qualities as a Counselor

1. If you were to seek out a counselor, what would you desire in one?

_____

_____

_____

_____

2. In each passage below, what quality do you discover about God? What does this quality mean in a counselor? (The references in parentheses are optional.)

25

Psalm 34:17-18 (James 4:8)

_____

_____

_____

_____

Psalm 139:7-10 (Proverbs 18:24; Matthew 28:20)

_____

_____

_____

_____

Psalm 147:4-5 (Isaiah 40:25-28; Proverbs 8:14)

_____

_____

_____

_____

Jeremiah 31:3 (Psalm 86:5; John 15:9)

_____

_____

_____

_____

Daniel 2:20-22 (Psalm 16:7; Ephesians 1:17; Colossians 2:2-3)

_____

_____

_____

_____

_____

Titus 1:2 (John 3:33; 1 John 1:5)

_____

_____

_____

_____

The Benefits of Jesus' Counsel

3. As you seek after Him "in whom are hidden all the treasures of wisdom and knowledge" (Colossians 2:3), what does He promise to do?

   Jeremiah 33:3 _____

   _____

   _____

   Hosea 6:3 _____

   _____

   _____

Matthew 7:7-8 _____

_____

_____

James 1:5 _____

_____

_____

4. In what situations or areas of your life do you desire counsel?

_____

_____

_____

5. Remembering how well Jesus Christ knows you, read John 1:3 and Ephesians 5:13-14.

   a. What can He specifically do for you when you are troubled or fearful and you do not know the cause of your feelings, or when you do not understand your pattern of behavior?

   _____

   _____

   _____

   _____

   b. In such circumstances, what do you need to do?

   _____

   _____

c. Specifically, what would you like the light of Christ to shine on and make known to you?

_____

_____

_____

d. As He reveals, He also heals. Record the results here, whether they happen immediately or over a period of time.

_____

_____

_____

_____

_____

6. Read Psalm 25:14, Proverbs 1:23, and Amos 4:13.

a. When what you are experiencing is confusing, what can the Lord do to help you understand His purpose in it?

_____

_____

_____

b. How would you describe your *typical* reaction when things are difficult to understand?

_____ Angry at God

_____ Angry with yourself or others

_____ Pleading with God to change things

_____ Looking for a way of escape

_____ Open to Him for His insight, counsel, and strength in the situation

_____ Other: _____

_____

_____

_____

c. Jesus' counsel can heal your fears and give you understanding. As you consider the verses given in this question, what is a good first step to take in confusing times? Do you need to do this now?

_____

_____

_____

_____

7. Read the following verses to identify another way in which His counsel is beneficial: Psalm 73:24; Proverbs 2:6-10; and Isaiah 58:11.

_____

_____

_____

_____

8. What is one tool the Lord uses to guide you? See Psalm 119:105.

_____

_____

9. Explain the point Jesus is making in Matthew 12:38-42.

_____

_____

_____

10. What advice is given to you in 2 Chronicles 18:4?

_____

_____

_____

_____

What Is Yours to Do?

11. What does God encourage you to do in Proverbs 23:12?

_____

_____

_____

12. To begin exploring ways your Wonderful Counselor can help when talking with someone, consider the verses below.

Psalm 139:4 and 141:3_____

_____

_____

Proverbs 22:17-21; Luke 12:11-12 _____

_____

_____

Proverbs 12:18,25 and 15:1,4,23 _____

_____

_____

How have you seen the Lord be this to you in the past?

_____

_____

_____

13. Since the Lord is the most creative Being, from whom you have received your creative nature, He can counsel you with unique ideas and approaches.

a. Which of your relationships need "new life," or at least some creativity?

_____

_____

b. What projects or responsibilities of yours need some creativity?

_____

_____

14. Turn to Colossians 3:16. What is a safeguard for you in giving as well as receiving His counsel?

_____

_____

_____

15. What are some avenues through which you can receive Jesus' counsel?

_____

_____

_____

_____

16. What difficulties do you experience in seeking God's wisdom and counsel?

_____

_____

_____

_____

What can you do about each one?

_____

_____

_____

_____

17. What can you do when you're unsure whether insight, wisdom, or direction is from the Lord?

_____

_____

_____

_____

18. Review question 4 and your responses.

    a. What steps will you take now in each situation or area of your life?

    _____

    _____

    _____

    _____

    _____

    _____

    b. Record the results here as they take place.

    _____

    _____

    _____

    _____

    _____

    _____

19. As Jesus Christ answers you and reveals His secret wisdom to you, what is to be your response, proclaimed by David in Psalm 16:7?

_____

_____

_____

_____

20. Write out and memorize Jeremiah 33:3. In memorizing God's Word, His truths take root in your heart and are available to help you in times of need.

_____

_____

_____

_____

Questions for Further Discussion

Question 3: What is your reaction to seeking counsel from one you cannot "see"? If you have difficulty with this, or if it's frustrating to you, what are some things you can do that would help?

Question 5: Read 1 Corinthians 2:6-10 and 16. What more do you discover that the Lord can do for you as your Counselor?

Question 6: What can keep you from doing this? Consider emotions as well as circumstances. Talk with the Lord about each one.

Question 8: Give an example in which He has used this to counsel you in the direction you should go. How do you think He could use this? What are some precautions it would be wise to take, or some guidelines that would be helpful in accepting the guidance of His Word?

Question 10: What got the Israelites into trouble in Joshua 9:14 as they looked only at how things appeared on the surface? What are some reasons you do not seek the counsel of the Lord? What can happen as a result of not seeking His counsel?

Question 12: In Proverbs 3:13-18, how does Solomon describe the one who has wisdom? Can you give an example of a time when the Lord gave you insight into the needs of another, the root of a problem, or steps one should take in handling a difficult situation? Is there a relationship for which you need this help today? Make your specific request of the Lord.

Question 13: Give an example of creativity He gave you in the past. How can you develop the habit of drawing on His creativity?

Question 14: How does this work? Is it "unspiritual" to seek professional help? Can God choose to work through this means?

Question 15: Why can the Lord give you proper counsel and guidance? Consider Psalm 139:1 and 1 Corinthians 13:12.

Question 19: Summarize your discoveries about this Wonderful Counselor and how you are experiencing Him in your life.

4
Immanuel

In the meaning of Jesus' name Immanuel, a truth is conveyed that has profound implications for each of us. Jesus desires to be Immanuel in whatever you are experiencing today. For further insight turn now to God's Word.

The Meaning of This Name

1. What are your needs today? Are you facing any difficulties? What emotions lie deep within?

_____

_____

_____

_____

_____

2. What is God's message to you in Christ's name Immanuel? Read Matthew 1:22-23.

_____

_____

_____

3. God's message in this name for Christ takes on meaning as we see who God is, recorded in the following passages.

1 Chronicles 29:10-13 _____

_____

_____

Psalm 103 _____

_____

_____

Isaiah 40:25-31 _____

_____

_____

Isaiah 41:4 _____

_____

_____

4. How can these discoveries about God help you in what you are experiencing today (see question 1)? Be specific.

_____

_____

_____

_____

_____

The Coming of Immanuel

5. In Matthew 1:22-23 you read that Christ was the fulfillment of a prophecy. What more do you learn about Him in these passages?

John 1:1-5 and 10-14 _____

_____

_____

Philippians 2:6-11 _____

_____

_____

Colossians 1:15-20 _____

_____

_____

Hebrews 1:1-4 _____

_____

_____

6. Read John 3:16-17, 13:1, and 1 John 4:9-10. What was God's motivation in sending Jesus?

_____

_____

_____

_____

7. What does this mean to you personally?

_____

_____

_____

_____

8. In addition to coming to earth many years ago, Jesus desires to come to you today. Read John 14:15-21 to find how this can be, since He no longer walks on earth.

_____

_____

_____

_____

9. Immanuel was with many people as He walked on earth, yet many did not recognize the truth of His presence. Often today He goes unrecognized as well. If you so desire, ask Him to open your eyes and give you an increased awareness of His presence with you. Look for Him now. Be open to Him in the future. Record here how and when you "see" Him with you.

_____

_____

_____

_____

_____

_____

The Lord Desires to Help You

10. As Immanuel, Jesus Christ is with you in your difficult times. Read Psalm 139:1-12.

   a. What can the "darkness" represent?

   _____

   _____

   _____

   b. When you feel hidden from God by darkness that enfolds you, what must you remember and claim in this passage?

   _____

   _____

   _____

11. What is Jesus' promise to you when you are facing difficulty? Consider Psalm 91:14-15, Isaiah 43:1-2, and Lamentations 3:19-24 and 55-57.

   _____

   _____

   _____

12. Because the Lord knows you intimately, He desires to help you deal with your fears.

   a. Identify any fears you may have—big or little, serious or "silly."

   _____

_____

_____

_____

b. In each passage below, what is God's personal promise to you about each fear?

Deuteronomy 31:8 _____

_____

_____

Psalm 34:4-5 _____

_____

_____

Isaiah 46:3-4 _____

_____

_____

c. Each time you are aware of a feeling of fear, recall God's promises to you. Write out one of His promises here and commit it to memory.

_____

_____

_____

_____

_____

13. Are you faced with making some decisions today? Are there some choices concerning the direction you should go? If so, identify those here.

_____

_____

_____

_____

Summarize God's promises to you in each verse or passage that follows.

Psalm 32:8 _____

_____

_____

Psalm 138:8 _____

_____

_____

Proverbs 3:5-6 _____

_____

_____

14. Read these verses to identify another time in which Jesus Christ is very much with you.

Isaiah 53:4 _____

_____

2 Corinthians 1:3-5 _____

_____

1 Peter 4:12-19 _____

_____

15. What is communicated to you in Psalm 38:9?

_____

_____

_____

How does this help you?

_____

_____

_____

16. In what ways are you suffering today? Bring each situation to
the Lord now. You don't have to explain how you are feeling,
or what you are experiencing. He knows completely. He
understands—and He cares! His Spirit even prays with you
and for you with sighs too deep for words (Romans 8:27). Let
Him minister to you now in your suffering and comfort you.
Record here ways in which you see Him help you.

_____

_____

_____

_____

_____

17. Have you felt alone in your suffering, whether it's emotional, physical, or mental? It seems no one else can completely understand what another is feeling deep within (see Proverbs 14:10). What hope is described in Proverbs 18:24?

_____

_____

_____

_____

18. Are Jesus' presence and love real enough to meet your deepest needs?

_____

_____

In times when you feel lonely, what is His promise to you?

Isaiah 54:10 _____

_____

Hosea 2:19-20 _____

_____

Romans 8:38-39 _____

_____

19. What does Jesus promise in Matthew 28:16-20?

_____

_____

_____

20. According to John 14:17, how can Jesus be with you always?

_____

_____

_____

_____

Is this true for everyone, or is there a choice each person needs to make first? Read Acts 2:38.

_____

_____

_____

21. Would you like for Jesus Christ to truly be "with you," to live in you by His Spirit, never to leave you or forsake you? What does He promise in Romans 10:8-13 and Revelation 3:20?

_____

_____

_____

_____

If you have not yet, but would like to invite Him to live within you, write out your request here now.

_____

_____

_____

22. As you take this step, Immanuel lives within you, with all His resources, to be to you all that He is. Personalize His promises in Hebrews 13:5.

_____

_____

_____

_____

23. What are the implications of Jesus' words in John 14:23?

_____

_____

_____

_____

24. Summarize what you have discovered and experienced in this study of the name Immanuel. Recall these truths day by day.

_____

_____

_____

_____

_____

_____

Questions for Further Discussion

Question 2: Before you became a Christian, what would it have meant to you if someone had said, "God is with you"? How do you think most people would respond? Why?

Question 3: Psalm 139 is another helpful passage.

Question 8: In what specific instances in the past have you been aware of God being with you?

Question 10: Are you experiencing any forms of darkness? What are some examples? In what specific ways can the truths of Psalm 139 help you today?

Question 11: You might also read Psalm 37:39-40, and 91:14-15, and Philippians 3:8-10. In times of difficulty, do you find it hard to turn to the Lord, or do such times cause you to seek Him? What usually are the results of your choice?

Question 12: The following passages are also encouraging: Isaiah 26:3 and 41:9-10, John 14:27, and Philippians 4:6-7.

Question 13: Additional promises are found in Psalm 25:4-12, Isaiah 30:21 and 48:16-17, and Jeremiah 29:11.

Question 14: First Peter 1:6-9 and 5:8-11 may be encouraging to someone in the group.

Question 20: Is this a new thought for you? What are your feelings and reactions?

5
The Bread of Life

As when talking about the Good Shepherd, Jesus again uses imagery familiar to His listeners in calling Himself the Bread of Life. By talking about bread, a staple food for life, He communicates many significant truths about Himself.

There are only three basic types of bread: yeast, quick, and flat. Herein is an analogy with the Trinity, of which Jesus is one of three Persons.

For truths that affect your life today, turn to God's Word to explore this name of Jesus.

The "Living Bread" in You

1. Read John 6:30-35 and 47-58. What is Jesus' main message in these passages?

   _____

   _____

   _____

   _____

2. For bread to give you life, what must you do with it? How does this apply to Jesus as the Bread of Life?

   _____

_____

_____

_____

3. If you have not received this Bread of Life, but would like to, write out your request here.

_____

_____

_____

_____

Manna in the Wilderness

4. In the passages from John 6, a conversation with the Jews, Jesus compares Himself to the manna God sent from heaven when the Israelites were wandering in the wilderness. What symbolism does this have for your situation today?

_____

_____

_____

_____

_____

5. What encouragement is there for you in Psalm 105:40?

_____

_____

6. Read Exodus 16:4.

   a. What was God's instruction to the Israelites about how often they were to gather the manna?

   _____

   _____

   b. What application does this instruction have for nurturing Jesus' life in you?

   _____

   _____

   _____

   _____

7. In John 6:57 Jesus refers to "the one who feeds on me."

   a. What does it mean to feed on Jesus?

   _____

   _____

   _____

   _____

   b. How is He emphasizing the instruction given in Exodus 16:4?

   _____

   _____

   _____

8. How is this instruction repeated in the prayer Jesus gave His disciples in Matthew 6:9-13?

_____

_____

_____

_____

9. Turn again to John 6:56. What is an important result of feeding on Jesus?

_____

_____

_____

Why is this vital? See John 15:4-7.

_____

_____

_____

_____

Hunger for This Living Bread

10. Do you sense within you a hunger that you're having difficulty satisfying? What are you hungry for, and how are you trying to satisfy that desire?

_____

_____

_____

_____

11. What does Jesus say about spiritual hunger in Matthew 5:6?

_____

_____

_____

_____

Explain how this will happen.

_____

_____

_____

_____

12. If you do not have this hunger for Jesus, who is your right-eousness, what can you do? Read Matthew 7:7-9.

_____

_____

_____

Write out your request here, if you'd like.

_____

_____

_____

13. What will you find to be true once your hunger is satisfied, according to Psalm 34:8?

_____

_____

_____

_____

14. What are your needs today that can be satisfied only by the Bread of Life?

_____

_____

_____

_____

_____

Ask the Lord to meet you in each one.

_____

_____

_____

_____

Record the results you see and experience.

_____

_____

_____

_____

_____

_____

15. What is Jesus' promise in John 6:35 as you come to Him with your needs?

_____

_____

_____

_____

Questions for Further Discussion

Question 1: Which phrases in John 1:1-4 and 11-14 communicate the same truths?

Question 7: Do you dislike this imagery? If so, ask God to help you accept it so that you can discover and apply the truths He is communicating.

Question 9: Realizing how important it is to feed on Christ daily, how will you do this? Be specific.

Question 10: Is it possible that some people might try to satisfy spiritual hunger with physical food? Why might that be true? In what other ways do Christians and non-Christians attempt to satisfy their hunger?

Question 13: How has Jesus "tasted good" in the past? How has He satisfied your needs?

6
The Rock

Life can be frightening. So many things can happen! We frequently hear or read of disasters. We personally know people who have experienced tragedy in their lives or their families' lives. And we know it could happen to us.

As we hear of severe "storms" that hit others' lives, we may wonder if we could survive a storm. Some people unfortunately do not survive emotionally—or sometimes physically. The suicide rate is escalating rapidly. We need help!

Help is available. For insight, turn to God's Word.

Your Rock in the Storms of Life

1. The imagery of a rock is used throughout Scripture. In the following verses, who is the Rock? What characteristics of that person are mentioned?

Genesis 49:24-25 _mighty strong leader Rock of Israel_

Deuteronomy 32:4 _his works are perfect his ways are just (steadfast) faithful – does no wrong_

Psalm 78:35 _Redeemer_

78:15-20 _living water from Rock_

35-39

Isaiah 26:4 _trustworthy_

the Rock, eternal

testimony the Lord emphasis

1 Corinthians 10:3-4 _____

Israel in desert

Ex 17:6 rock   thirst

Ex 20:8 rock

2. In what ways will God be your Rock, according to the following passages?

Psalm 34 _____ _protects_

delivers from troubles

saves those crushed in spirit

Psalm 73:21-24 _____

hold me, steadfast.

Romans 8:35-39 _____

conqueror - overcomer

3. Read the parable in Matthew 7:24-27.

   a. What should you do in order to survive the storms that come your way?

   _____

   _____

58

_____

_____

   b. If your foundation is built on Jesus Christ, what will be the outcome of even the worst of storms?

_____

_____

_____

4. What additional encouragement do you find in 2 Samuel 22:1-4 and Psalm 27:5?

_____

_____

_____

Express your praise to the Lord.

_____

_____

_____

5. What are you going through right now?

_____

_____

_____

_____

What storms do you fear in the future?

_____

_____

_____

6. What can God do with even the most tragic occurrence? See Romans 8:28.

_____

_____

_____

_____

Living Water from the Rock

7. In the Old Testament God performed miracles to communicate some truths pertaining to Christ who was to come. What did God do in Exodus 17:6, referred to also in Psalm 105:41?

EX 20:8
_____

_____

_____

8. Read John 4:10,14, and 7:37. What does Christ your Rock give you?

living water – to dry soul
_____
quench thirst
_____

_____

9. What invitation does He extend to you in Isaiah 55:1-3 and Revelation 22:17?

_____

_____

_____

_____

10. What are you thirsty for today? God desires to give of Himself to you to satisfy your deepest needs.

_____

_____

_____

11. Read John 7:38-39.

   a. As Jesus fills you with Himself, what then happens?

   _____

   _____

   _____

   _____

   b. Who around you may need this living water flowing through you from the Rock? What can you do?

   _____

   _____

   _____

Go to the Rock

12. What is David's request in Psalm 61:2?

never be shaken

fortress

Why does he desire this? See Psalm 62:1-2.

need rest

shaken

13. Is Christ your Rock, the foundation for your life?

   a. If not, but you would like Him to be, write your request
   here.

   b. If He is, recall how He has been your foundation as storms
   have hit. Be specific.

14. If you're not firmly established on this Rock, how can you become more firmly rooted so that heavy winds and rains won't cause you to fall?

_____

_____

_____

_____

15. As you seek to know Christ in deeper, more satisfying ways, and to be more firmly grounded on Him as the foundation of your life, what is His promise to you in Matthew 7:7-8? Claim this now.

_____

_____

_____

Questions for Further Discussion

Question 3: Can you give an example of someone in whom you saw these truths illustrated?

Question 4: How have you experienced this? What have you learned from past experiences that you will apply in the midst of another storm, should one come your way?

Question 10: Why does God desire to satisfy your deepest needs, according to Jeremiah 31:3, Zephaniah 3:17, and John 15:9?

Question 11: Explain what it means to have streams of living water flow from within you, and give an example. What else does the Lord give us from the Rock, recorded in Deuteronomy 32:13-14 and Psalm 81:16? What does this mean very practically in your relationship with Him?

7
Sun of Righteousness

Sun of Righteousness is the last name given to Jesus Christ in the Old Testament. It's a name with a promise, and is full of meaning. To tap its depths is challenging, stimulating, and exciting. Experiencing the Lord as the Sun of Righteousness will brighten your countenance and expand your horizon.

Truths of the Sun

1. Read Malachi 4:2. It's interesting to note that God refers to Jesus as the *Sun* of Righteousness rather than the *Son* of Righteousness. God created the sun (see Genesis 1:16) and uses His creation to reveal Himself (Romans 1:20). What facts or characteristics of the sun can you think of that give insight into Jesus' divine nature?

_____

_____

_____

_____

_____

_____

2. According to Genesis 1:15, what does the light of the earth's sun do?

_____

_____

_____

How essential is sunlight to life?

_____

_____

_____

3. How is Jesus described in the following verses? What attributes of His light are given?

John 1:4-5,9 _____

_____

John 8:12 _____

_____

Hebrews 1:3 _____

_____

4. How do the facts about the sun apply to Jesus Christ?

_____

_____

_____

_____

5. Genesis 1:16 refers to two luminaries that God created. One is the source of light—our sun. The other—the moon—has no light of its own, but rather reflects the light of the sun. How do these facts apply to your relationship with Jesus Christ, considering Matthew 5:14-16?

_____

_____

_____

_____

6. What are the implications of the following facts in your relationship with Jesus Christ? How can you apply each to your life?

   a. The sun is the center of our solar system. Everything revolves around it. Before this truth was discovered by Copernicus, people thought the solar system revolved around the earth. However, by holding to this principle, all facts did not compute properly. That led to the discovery that the sun is the center (the "heliocentric principle").

   _____

   _____

   _____

   _____

   b. The sun has such brilliance that you cannot look at it with the naked eye.

   _____

   _____

   _____

c. The light of the sun brings an added dimension of beauty, clarity, and color to God's creation.

_____

_____

_____

_____

d. The sun is a constant energy source.

_____

_____

_____

_____

7. Now consider the fact that the sun is constant, even when you can't see it!

a. How does Jesus Christ fulfill this truth according to

Psalm 73:23 _____

_____

Psalm 77:19-20 _____

_____

Psalm 139:7-12 _____

_____

Hebrews 13:8 _____

_____

b. How can these verses help you? What will your response be
    now on "cloudy" days? Be specific.

    _____

    _____

    _____

    _____

c. Select one of the verses above to memorize. Write it out
    here.

    _____

    _____

    _____

    _____

8. Read Malachi 3:2-3.

    a. The sun is a ball of fire. How is the Lord described?

        _____

        _____

        _____

    b. What will He do as such?

        _____

        _____

        _____

c. What will be the effect of exposure to the Sun of Righteousness?

_____

_____

_____

9. Although you are righteous in God's sight when Christ comes to live in you (Romans 3:21-24), the Lord desires to have His righteousness exhibited in your life more and more clearly (2 Corinthians 3:18). What does He use in your life to bring this about? Consider Hebrews 12:11 and 1 Peter 1:6-7.

_____

_____

_____

10. Can any person be righteous in and of his or her own efforts? See Romans 3:9-10.

_____

_____

11. How are your righteous acts described in Isaiah 64:6?

_____

_____

12. Where does your true righteousness lie then? Examine Isaiah 45:24 and 1 Corinthians 1:30.

_____

_____

13. Turn to Romans 6:13 and 12:1 to learn what your part is in growing in righteousness.

_____

_____

_____

14. Read again Malachi 3:2-3. Do you desire to be an offering in righteousness, pleasing to the Lord? Ask Him to burn out all impurities within you by His fire. Honestly express your feelings and desires to Him. He knows and understands, and will meet you where you are in His love.

_____

_____

_____

_____

_____

15. Read Malachi 4:1-2 and 2 Peter 3:10-13. What event is spoken of here?

_____

_____

16. What healing is being spoken of in Malachi 4:2? See Isaiah 53:4-5 and 1 Peter 2:24.

_____

_____

_____

17. As described in the following verses, what will the condition be of those who belong to the Lord?

Malachi 4:2 _____

_____

John 10:10 _____

_____

John 15:11 and 16:22 _____

_____

1 John 3:2-3 _____

_____

18. In what ways would you like to experience more of the Sun of Righteousness? Be specific. Then pray to the Lord about your requests.

_____

_____

_____

_____

Questions for Further Discussion

Question 3: What do you think the word *darkness* in John refers to? Is there any other kind of darkness you are experiencing today? Since God's Word (Jesus) drives out darkness and gives light, what is your specific request to Him?

Question 5: What does this discovery say to you regarding your own efforts to create "light" in your own life?

Question 6c: What happens when light hits a prism? How does this illustrate what happens when the light of the Sun of Righteousness shines on you? What must be true of the prism first? What feelings does this produce in you?

Question 7: What is your usual response when you cannot "see" the Lord or feel His warmth?

Question 8: What does it mean to be refined like gold and silver? How is the Lord described in Hebrews 12:28-29? What have been your thoughts and feelings when you have experienced the heat of the Refiner?

Question 11: What is your reaction to this statement? How do you try to make yourself "righteous"?

Question 12: What name for Christ is found in Jeremiah 23:6 and 33:16?

Question 13: What parallels do you see between the growth of a plant and the growth of righteousness in your life?

Question 15: What are your reactions as you think of "the day of the Lord"?

Question 16: Is this healing of your broken, sinful condition not received in any measure until the day of the Lord? What is implied in passages such as Isaiah 48:18, 2 Corinthians 3:18, and Hebrews 10:14?

Question 17: What are the psalmist's expressions of joy in the following verses: Psalm 4:6-7, 7:17, and 16:2 and 11? How is the kingdom of God described in Romans 14:17? Is this the way those who walk with Christ in His kingdom are usually seen? Why? What is your usual source of joy? What can you do to nurture your joy in the Lord? Be specific.

8
Your Redeemer

The name Redeemer is a wonderful word of hope! This hope applies to ourselves as well as to our circumstances. In the midst of difficulty we can call on our Redeemer, and He will act to bring good out of the situation. The messages given to us through this name are practical and exciting. To explore them, turn to God's Word.

Redeemer of Your Life

1. Look up the definition of *redeem* in a dictionary.

_____

_____

_____

_____

2. Why do you need a redeemer? Consider Romans 3:23.

_____

_____

_____

_____

3. Why is Jesus your Redeemer? See Ephesians 1:7 and Colossians 1:13-14.

_____

_____

_____

_____

4. Remembering the definition of redeem, what does it mean that Jesus Christ has redeemed you?

_____

_____

_____

5. What identity do you have then, according to Isaiah 62:12 and 1 Peter 2:9-10?

_____

_____

_____

_____

6. Read Psalm 107:1-2.

    a. How should you respond to the gift of redemption?

    _____

    _____

    _____

b. Who will share your joy if you tell them what Christ has done for you?

_____

_____

c. Express your thanks to Christ for your redeemed identity.

_____

_____

_____

_____

7. In addition to giving you salvation, what does Jesus desire to make of your life? Consider John 10:10 and Ephesians 3:20.

_____

_____

_____

How is He doing this in your life today?

_____

_____

_____

_____

8. Realizing Jesus' desire, what are your requests of Him? Be specific. Then watch in anticipation as you yield to His Spirit and allow Him to work.

_____

77

_____

_____

_____

_____

_____

9. Read Luke 18:18-27.

   a. What message is Jesus communicating?

   _____

   _____

   _____

   _____

   b. Who do you claim this truth for? Pray now for each person.

   _____

   _____

10. Read about Saul in Acts 7:57-8:1 and 9:1-22. How is he an encouragement to you concerning those you care about and are praying for?

    _____

    _____

    _____

    _____

Redeemer of Situations and Circumstances

11. Jesus is the Redeemer, moment by moment, as we walk through our days. How is this illustrated in 1 Samuel 17:1-11 and 32-50?

_____

_____

_____

_____

What "giants" are you facing? Are there any ways in which you feel "under attack"?

_____

_____

_____

_____

How can you ward off these or stand against them?

_____

_____

_____

_____

Is there a specific situation you would like to give to the Lord now for Him to redeem? Describe it and pray about it.

_____

_____

_____

_____

12. What is Jeremiah's message in Lamentations 3:52-58?

_____

_____

_____

_____

What present circumstance, if any, can you identify as your "depths of the pit"?

_____

_____

_____

_____

13. What are you assured of in Lamentations 3:19-26?

_____

_____

_____

14. As you see Jesus work in your life or the lives of others, what can you say with assurance, as recorded in Job 19:25?

_____

_____

_____

15. Express your praise to your Redeemer.

   _____

   _____

   _____

   _____

Questions for Further Discussion

Question 2: What name is given to God in Isaiah 47:4 and 54:5?

Question 6: How is this supported by Romans 10:9-10?

Question 9: The Lord desires to redeem others' lives as He does yours. How is this encouraging to you?

Question 10: Who can you think of who illustrates the truth of Jesus as Redeemer?

Question 11: How can you nurture a faith in God like David had in his situation? When a good situation goes awry, what can you do?

Question 13: How have you seen Jesus redeem circumstances in your life in the past? How can that help you today?

9
Rose of Sharon

Rose of Sharon, a beautiful name with a special message, is found in Song of Songs 2:1 (Song of Solomon). The lover, usually considered to represent Jesus Christ, is referred to as "a rose of Sharon."

Henry Gariepy, in *Portraits of Christ,* gives insight into the significance of this name. Rose of Sharon is suggestive of the fragrance of Christ's life. Gariepy writes about some roses that are found in a valley of Rumania: "Roses are grown for the Vienna market in great profusion and with much distillation of fragrance. We are told that if you were to visit that valley at the time of the rose crop, wherever you would go the rest of the day, the fragrance you would carry with you would betray where you had been."

He goes on to say that "there is a beautiful parable given us by the Persian poet and moralist, Saadi. The poet was given a bit of ordinary clay. The clay was so redolent with sweet perfume that its fragrance filled all the room.

"'What are you, musk or ambergris?' he questioned.

"'I am neither,' it answered. 'I am just a bit of common clay.'

"'From where then do you have this rare perfume?' the poet asked.

"'I have companied all the summer with the rose,' it replied."

Henry Gariepy then comments, "We are just bits of the common clay of humanity. But if we company with the One who is the Rose of Sharon . . . something of the fragrance of His life will pass into ours. Then we will be a freshening and a sweetening influence to the world around us."[1]

The Source of Fragrance

1. Turn to Song of Songs 1:3. How does the beloved react to the name of her lover? Why do you think she feels that way?

   _____

   _____

   _____

   _____

2. Read 2 Corinthians 2:14-16.

   a. What fragrance does God desire to come from your life?

      _____

      _____

      _____

   b. How is Jesus described in John 1:4 and 14:6?

      _____

      _____

      _____

      _____

   c. In what two ways is the fragrance described?

      _____

      _____

      _____

d. What are the results of Christ's fragrance in your life? Can you give some examples?

_____

_____

_____

_____

3. In John 15:1-5 you read how the life of Christ flowing through you also produces fruit that gives off a fragrance, as is expressed in Song of Songs 2:13. So then, what is another result of His fragrance in your life, according to John 15:8 and Philippians 1:11?

_____

_____

_____

_____

4. Is such a fragrance forced on others? How do you think people become aware of it?

_____

_____

_____

5. For God's desired results to be achieved, what must be the qualities of His fragrance? Consider Galatians 5:22-23.

_____

_____

Express your heart to the Lord concerning this in your life.

_____

_____

_____

_____

6. What is the Lord's response to your Christ-like fragrance, expressed in Song of Songs 4:10? Meditate on this today.

_____

_____

_____

7. In Exodus 30:34-35 the Lord gives Moses instructions for making a fragrant blend of incense. How does that apply to what the Lord desires for your life?

_____

_____

_____

_____

How to Have Christ's Fragrance

8. Do you think the fragrance God desires from your life is something you can manufacture? How do Christians sometimes try?

_____

_____

_____

_____

9. Remember that true fragrance belongs to Jesus Christ. To be
fragrant yourself, what is necessary initially? Consider John
14:17 and Colossians 1:27.

_____

_____

_____

_____

10. Do you have His life and fragrance within? If you do not but
would like to, or if you would like to be absolutely certain,
simply ask Him to come and live within you—and He promises He will! Record your thoughts here.

_____

_____

_____

_____

_____

11. Recall the story of the roses in Rumania.

a. How can it apply to the strength of the fragrance of the
Rose of Sharon in your life?

_____

_____

_____

b. What must you do? Consider Christ's example of His relationship with His Father, revealed in Matthew 14:22-23 and Mark 1:35. Be specific.

_____

_____

_____

c. How often is perfume applied? How does this relate to the perfume of Christ in your life?

_____

_____

_____

_____

12. What additional insight do you receive from 2 Corinthians 3:18 and Ephesians 3:17-19 as to how His fragrance becomes strong within?

_____

_____

_____

_____

13. According to the following passages, who spreads the fragrance of Christ in your life?

Song of Songs 4:16 with John 3:8 _____

_____

_____

Luke 14:10 _____

_____

2 Corinthians 2:14 _____

_____

1 Timothy 5:25 _____

_____

14. If the fragrance of your life were to be bottled, what might it be called? What would you like it to be called?

_____

_____

Are they one and the same? What is the reason?

_____

_____

_____

How Your Fragrance Can Be Spoiled

15. In Song of Songs 2:13 you read that the fruit of your life produces a fragrance.

a. What admonition in Song of Songs 2:15 could consequently apply to you?

_____

_____

_____

b. Consider Hebrews 12:1 as you explain what these "little foxes" represent.

_____

_____

_____

c. What little foxes are perhaps spoiling the fragrance of your life, and what can you do about each? Be specific.

_____

_____

_____

_____

_____

d. If confession is necessary, take time to do this now. What is God's promise to you in 1 John 1:9?

_____

_____

_____

16. Summarize from this lesson what things are essential for your life to spread the fragrance of Christ daily. Are you willing to do these things?

_____

_____

_____

17. Select a verse from this lesson that was especially meaningful to you. Write it here and commit it to memory. As you do, open yourself to Jesus Christ. Let Him fill you with the fragrance of His life.

_____

_____

_____

_____

Questions for Further Discussion

Question 2: How does Song of Songs 2:1 support the description of Jesus? Why do people have different reactions to the fragrance?

Question 3: What are some other results you might want, which could take away from God's desired results? Which ones do you personally struggle with?

Question 4: Are you aware of your own fragrance? Have you met someone in whom you were aware of this fragrance of Christ immediately? Why were you?

Question 8: What are you cautioned not to do in Proverbs 25, verses 6,7, and 27, and Matthew 6:1-3? How do Christians do this today? Why is this tempting to do? What are some possible results of trying to spread your own fragrance? Can you relate a time in which you did this? How did you feel? Was the result satisfying?

Question 9: What are the differences between manufactured perfume and the fragrance of Christ? How does Jesus Christ, including His fragrance, come into your life? Consider the imagery in Revelation 3:20.

Question 11: Can you give an example from your own life or someone you know who illustrates this truth? In *The Way of the Heart* Henri Nouwen writes, "St. Anthony spent twenty years in isolation [apart with Christ]. When he left it he took his solitude with him and shared it with all who came to him. Those who saw him described him as balanced, gentle, and caring. He had become so Christlike, so radiant with God's love, that his entire being was ministry."[2] What message is there here for you?

Question 13: How does this work practically? How have you seen the Lord spread the fragrance of Christ either in your life or in the life of another? Think about the differences the fragrance of Christ would make in your home or at work or in your community.

Question 15: Paraphrase Ecclesiastes 10:1. How have you seen this to be true? What can keep you from stopping those little foxes?

(Sometimes they're so cute, so lovable and entertaining!) What help can Jesus' presence within you give in overcoming these intruders? See Hebrews 4:15-16. Ask Him now for His help.

Question 16: Do you think there are any "shortcuts" to acquiring the fragrance of Christ? Why or why not?

Notes
1. Henry Gariepy, *Portraits of Christ* (Old Tappan, New Jersey: Fleming H. Revell Company, 1974), pages 21-22.
2. Henri J.M. Nouwen, *The Way of the Heart* (New York: Ballantine Books, 1981), page 18.

10
Your Bridegroom

As He walked on earth, Jesus Christ often referred to Himself as the Bridegroom, and to us, His people (male and female), as His bride. The marriage relationship is used throughout Scripture to represent the spiritual relationship our Lord desires with each of us—that of intimacy, love, and oneness.

Opening ourselves to Christ as our spiritual husband brings us into an experience of love such as we have never known before. Transcending the sexual nature of earthly marriages, Christ relates to us as male or female with a higher, purer love. This surpasses all the human relationships we can know, even as satisfying and fulfilling as those can be! The full and perfect love of God truly satisfies our deepest longings and needs. Therefore, let us put aside our maleness or femaleness and see Christ the Lord as our husband who desires true oneness with us.

The Bridegroom and His Bride

1. What qualities are desirable in a husband?

_____

_____

_____

_____

2. What qualities are found in the Lord? Look up the following verses.

   a. Psalm 32:1-5 _____

   _____

   b. Psalm 119:160 _____

   _____

   c. Psalm 136:1 _____

   _____

   d. Psalm 146:6 _____

   _____

   e. Jeremiah 31:3 and Zephaniah 3:17 _____

   _____

   _____

   f. Matthew 11:28-29 _____

   _____

3. How does Jesus refer to Himself in Matthew 9:14-15?

   _____

   _____

4. In John 1:29 Jesus is called the Lamb of God. With that in mind, explain what is happening in Revelation 19:7-9.

   _____

   _____

_____

_____

What are your thoughts and feelings about that event?

_____

_____

_____

_____

_____

5. Read Hosea 2:19-20. Visualize Jesus facing you at a church altar. Hear Him personalize these vows of His to you. Then repeat them to Him, concluding with "and I acknowledge you as my true Husband and Lord."
   What do you experience in doing this?

_____

_____

_____

_____

Being a Bride

6. What does the Lord desire for you to do daily, expressed by Jesus in John 15:9?

_____

_____

How can you do this?

_____

_____

_____

Write out John 15:9. Commit it to memory. Repeat it often to yourself during the day. Meditate on Jesus' love. Practice resting in it and enjoying it.

_____

_____

_____

Record your discoveries as you do this.

_____

_____

_____

_____

7. Think of ways in which a woman today prepares herself to be a wife her husband will delight in. (Consider all areas, not just the physical.) Relate these ideas to the spiritual as you list some things you can do to be pleasing to Christ.

_____

_____

_____

_____

8. Think of yourself as a "bride" to be presented to Christ. What effect does this have on the areas below?

a. The effort you make in spending time with Him each day

_____

_____

_____

b. Your anticipation of eternity

_____

_____

_____

c. The strength you have not to give in to temptation

_____

_____

_____

d. Your self-image

_____

_____

_____

9. What does Paul claim about your spiritual Husband in Philippians 4:19?

_____

_____

10. How can Christ as your Husband help you in the following experiences? Be specific and practical. Remember to look for Him in the days that follow.

a. When lonely

_____

_____

_____

b. When deep needs are unmet by another; for example, the need to be understood

_____

_____

_____

c. When you need a provider

_____

_____

_____

d. When you need a companion

_____

_____

_____

e. When you need to know you have worth

_____

_____

_____

f. When you need someone to share your dreams and joys

_____

_____

_____

g. Other (Be specific in your personal needs today!)

_____

_____

_____

_____

Jesus Your Husband

11. You read in John 15:9 that Christ wants you to remain in His love. He desires a delightful intimacy with you.

    a. Does your awareness of your own unworthiness of such a love hold you back? Read and meditate on Ephesians 2:4-9. What truths in this passage can help you accept the relationship that Christ desires?

    _____

    _____

    _____

    _____

101

b. Do you fear intimacy with the Lord? If so, identify the reasons why.

_____

_____

_____

_____

According to John 8:32 and 36, and 1 John 4:18, what can free you from these fears?

_____

_____

_____

_____

Therefore, what will be important for you to do?

_____

_____

_____

12. An important aspect of this love relationship with Jesus Christ is what He desires from you, His beloved. See the following verses.

Matthew 22:37-38 _____

_____

John 14:21 _____

_____

Ephesians 6:24 _____

_____

13. Song of Songs symbolically represents our love relationship with the Lord. Read 1:2-4, 2:1-4, 2:8-13, and 4:9-16. Which expressions of both the Lover (the Lord) and the beloved (you) are meaningful to you? You may want to personalize them specifically, based on your relationship with Him.

a. Expressions of your heart to the Lord

_____

_____

_____

_____

_____

_____

b. Expressions of the Lord to you

_____

_____

_____

_____

_____

_____

14. In Song of Songs 5:16, after the maiden has described the one she loves, she concludes by exclaiming, "He is altogether

lovely. This is my lover, this my friend." In closing now, write your own expression of love and praise to the Lord.

_____

_____

_____

_____

_____

Questions for Further Discussion

Question 2: What is your response to your discoveries in these verses? Meditate on all these qualities of Christ. In what ways could your experience of His qualities be healing to you?

Here are additional verses for each quality: a. Psalm 103:10-12 and 1 John 1:9; b. Titus 1:2 and 1 John 1:5; c. Psalm 100:5 and Luke 18:19; d. 1 Corinthians 1:9 and Hebrews 10:23; e. Psalm 145:17 and John 15:9; f. Isaiah 40:11 and Hosea 2:14.

Question 3: What testimony did John the Baptist give in John 3:27-30 concerning Jesus Christ? In Matthew 22:1-3 what imagery is used to portray Jesus' role among believers?

Question 4: Why has the bride been given fine linen to wear?

Question 5: Describe what an ideal marriage relationship is intended to be like.

Question 6: What choices do you have in this?

Question 7: What can you do to help the Church, when it is presented to Christ, to be a bride in whom He will delight?

Question 9: Do you think it is an overstatement that Jesus Christ can meet every need? What about your sexual, material, and emotional needs? Can God truly be as a husband to you? (Is His ability to provide for your needs through other channels a consideration?)

Do you think all of a person's needs can be met in one's mate? Do you think another person can totally understand what you're feeling and share completely your experiences? Why or why not? Are there dangers inherent in expecting one person or people in general to meet your needs? Explain.

Question 11: Is there a danger of becoming "exclusive" in your relationship with the Lord? Compare this to a couple's love. As you experience the fullness of God's love, what does He desire for you to do? (Consider the scriptural principle, "blessed to be a blessing.")

Question 13: One of the highest forms of a love relationship is enjoying being in one another's presence, delighting in each other. How can you nurture this relationship with the Lord? Be specific.

11
Commander of the Lord's Army

War, unfortunately, is a reality people have always lived with. We read of battles within countries and between nations. We fear another world war. How to be adequately prepared to defend our country in case of attack is an important issue facing our nation.

Yet there is another war that has been waged from the beginning of time. It does not make the headlines, but is every bit as real and involves every individual. It is not between nations, but between kingdoms. It is taking place in the spiritual realm, truly a critical and significant struggle. There is a battle actively being fought between the "dominion of darkness" and the "kingdom of light" (Colossians 1:13).

To learn all you can about this real war and to see what hope is ours through Jesus Christ, our Commander, turn to God's Word. If there is any resistance within you, consciously or subconsciously, to consider such an issue, ask the Lord to free you from this and to lead you into discoveries from His Word.

The Two Powers

1. Read Ephesians 6:10-12 and identify the two sides in this spiritual warfare.

   _____

   _____

   _____

2. How is Satan described in the following verses?

Genesis 3:1 _____

_____

John 8:44 _____

_____

John 10:9-10 _____

_____

2 Corinthians 11:14-15 _____

_____

3. On the other hand, what qualities and attributes belong to God? Consider 1 Chronicles 29:10-12.

_____

_____

_____

The Nature of this War

4. What do you think each side is striving for? Read 1 Timothy 2:3-4 and Revelation 12:9.

_____

_____

_____

_____

5. Satan usually attacks a person's vulnerable areas.

   a. How does he generally attack you? Does he put self-condemning thoughts in your mind? Does he whisper lies about God? Does he discourage you in your work?

   _____

   _____

   _____

   _____

   _____

   b. How does being aware of his tactics help you?

   _____

   _____

   _____

   _____

   _____

   c. Are you experiencing Satan's attack today, or feeling the oppression of spirit that comes from him? (If you're not sure, the Lord can reveal this to you if you ask Him.) Claim victory over Satan through Jesus Christ within you!

   _____

   _____

   _____

   _____

6. What actions are you to take towards God and against Satan?

Ephesians 6:11 _____

_____

James 4:7-8 _____

_____

1 Peter 5:8-9 _____

_____

What choices are yours? _____

_____

_____

Equipped for Battle

7. Read 2 Corinthians 10:4 and describe the weapons you are equipped with.

_____

_____

_____

8. In Ephesians 6:10-18 you will discover specific provisions God gives you in battling Satan, which are at your disposal.

a. Whose power enables you to fight the battle? Why is this important to recognize?

_____

110

_____

_____

b. What is Paul's instruction to you regarding this armor?

_____

_____

_____

c. Identify each piece of armor, explaining the function of it. Keep in mind your vulnerable areas and think of how you can use each piece in battling Satan.

_____

_____

_____

_____

_____

_____

_____

_____

_____

_____

_____

The Confidence You Have

9. What thought in 2 Chronicles 20:15 will help you in the midst of the battle, whatever form it takes?

    _____

    _____

    _____

10. During times of struggle, hope may seem dim.

    a. At such times what do you need to do, according to Psalm 27:13-14 and 56:3-4?

        _____

        _____

        _____

        _____

    b. As you wait on the Lord, what will He do for you? Turn to Isaiah 40:29-31.

        _____

        _____

        _____

11. When Satan attacks, what else does Christ do for you that should give you confidence and encouragement? See Luke 22:31-32 and Hebrews 7:25.

    _____

    _____

_____

_____

12. As you suffer at the hand of Satan, what can you be confident of, as promised in the following verses?

Job 23:10 _____

_____

2 Thessalonians 1:4-5 _____

_____

James 1:2-4,12 _____

_____

1 Peter 4:1-2 _____

_____

1 Peter 4:12-14 _____

_____

13. In your suffering, of what can you be assured?

John 10:28 _____

_____

1 Corinthians 15:57 _____

_____

2 Thessalonians 3:3 _____

_____

Claim these promises even when you can't "see" or "feel" the Lord's presence.

14. In Scripture, the phrase *king of Babylon* often symbolizes Satan.

    a. With that in mind, what promise does the Lord give in Jeremiah 42:11?

    _____

    _____

    _____

    _____

    b. Which thought in 1 John 4:4 will you remember when you feel under attack?

    _____

    _____

    _____

    _____

15. How can you apply to your life the convictions expressed in Psalm 27:1-3 and 55:16-18?

    _____

    _____

    _____

    _____

    _____

The Outcome of This War

16. Whose kingdom will be established for eternity? See 1 Corinthians 15:24 and Revelation 11:15.

   _____

   _____

   How does knowledge of the outcome help you today? What differences will this make in your life?

   _____

   _____

   _____

   _____

17. In conclusion, write out 1 Corinthians 15:57. Commit this verse to memory and claim it whenever Satan attempts to attack you.

   _____

   _____

   _____

   _____

Questions for Further Discussion

Question 1: Are such thoughts about a spiritual battle new to you? What is your response to such a concept, and why? Who is head of the Lord's army, as stated in Joel 2:11? Read in Joshua 5:13-15 the interesting account of Joshua's encounter with the Commander of the Lord's army.

Question 2: You might also consider 2 Thessalonians 2:9-10 and Revelation 13:11-13.

How would you describe the devil? What concept of him do people generally hold, do you think? For those who choose to ignore his reality, do you think "ignorance is bliss"?

For study on the origin of Satan, if you have questions along this line, consider Isaiah 14:12-15 and Ezekiel 28:12-19, both of which refer symbolically to him. Also see Jesus' statement in Luke 10:18.

Question 4: How do these discoveries increase your awareness and sensitivity to what is going on in our world and in your own life? Be specific.

Dostoevski has said, "The devil fights against God, and the field of battle is man's heart."

Question 8: According to Romans 12:12 and 14, who actually embodies this full set of armor? What does that mean to you? How can the name Jesus be effective in rebuking Satan? How do you see Jesus obtain victory over Satan in his temptations in the wilderness, recorded in Matthew 4:1-11? How is the use of this weapon emphasized in 1 John 2:14? Can you relate an experience in using this armor, being specific in how you used it? If not, give an example of how you would use it during a time of "attack." How can you use this armor today?

Question 10: What is God's promise to you in 1 Peter 5:10-11? What has been your experience in this?

Question 12: These truths give us insight as to why the Lord allows this. Consider Joseph's perspective on his betrayal by his brothers in Genesis 45:5-8, along with Romans 8:28. In the midst of difficulty, then, of what are you assured? Can you give an example of how the Lord has used suffering in your life in the past? How can this help you now?

Question 14: For scriptural support, see Revelation 14:8, 16:19, 17:5, 18:2, and 18:21. Do you need to claim the promise in Jeremiah for your own life?

Question 16: What actually was accomplished by Christ on the cross and in His resurrection from the dead? Explain, considering John 10:28 and 12:30-31, Colossians 2:13-15, Hebrews 2:14-15, 1 Peter 3:22, and 1 John 3:8. How do these passages help you regarding those you love who also know Christ? Claim this now for each one.

12
Jesus

The name Jesus carries with it peace and power. It soothes and convicts. It is held in highest honor. Paul says in Philippians 2:9 that it is "the name that is above every name." Close your eyes and repeat the name Jesus several times. What do you discover? As you complete this chapter, you will find that there truly is something about that name.

Some consider Jesus to be Christ's only name (the others being titles), since it was given by divine command before His birth. An angel of the Lord said Mary's child was to be called Jesus "because he will save his people from their sins" (Matthew 1:21). Thus the name means "Savior." In examining the syllables in the word *Jesus,* this is also clear. According to Dr. Herbert Lockyer in *All the Divine Names and Titles in the Bible,* the letters *JE* represent the word *Jehovah,* indicating that Jesus is God. The syllable *SUS* is a derivative of names meaning "help." *Jesus* therefore means "the help of God" or "the salvation of God."[1] It is the most frequently used name, appearing in the New Testament over 700 times.

As in the preceding chapters, examining the name simply leads you to a Person. As you explore all that is in the name Jesus, may you see Him more clearly and experience Him more intimately as Friend, Savior, and Lord. May the Person of Christ capture your heart and fully become the devotion of your life.

Who Jesus Is

1. In order to understand why His name accomplishes all that the Bible claims, it is important to establish accurately who

Jesus is. What truths about Him are revealed in the following verses?

John 1:1-4,10-14 _____

_____

_____

_____

John 14:6 _____

_____

_____

John 20:31 _____

_____

_____

2. Read the description of Jesus given in Colossians 1:15-20.

a. List all that Jesus is and has done.

_____

_____

_____

_____

_____

_____

120

b. Which statements are most meaningful in your life today?

_____

_____

_____

_____

Life Through His Name

3. According to Matthew 1:21 and Acts 4:12, what is yours through Jesus' name?

_____

_____

_____

4. The reason this is possible is found in 1 Timothy 2:5-6. What has Jesus done for you, and what is His role now?

_____

_____

_____

_____

5. Your salvation has another dimension, found only in Jesus' name.

   a. To explain what this is, read Acts 10:43 and 1 Corinthians 6:11.

_____

_____

_____

b. Talk with Jesus regarding anything (big or small) that is keeping you from experiencing the fullness of life Christ desires for you. Accept the total cleansing that He gives.

_____

_____

_____

_____

The Power in His Name

6. Read Jesus' prayer recorded in John 17:11-12. What is another dimension of the power of His name? How will you benefit?

_____

_____

_____

_____

_____

7. What do you learn from Matthew 12:18-21 about the name of Jesus in relation to the nations?

_____

_____

_____

8. What do you discover and conclude about using the power of Jesus' name? Examine the following passages.

Mark 9:39-41 _____

_____

Acts 3:6-8, 16 _____

_____

Acts 4:7-12 _____

_____

Acts 5:28, 40-42 _____

_____

9. Read about the misuse of Jesus' name in Acts 19:11-20. What does this passage communicate to you?

_____

_____

_____

_____

10. To effectively pray or speak or act in the name of Jesus, what is necessary, and why? Explain by considering John 15:4-5 and 7.

_____

_____

_____

_____

What will be the result? Read 1 Corinthians 2:10 and 16.

_____

_____

_____

_____

11. Read John 2:11 and 20:30-31.

   a. What is Jesus' purpose in performing miracles? For insight, consider the term John uses in referring to Christ's miracles.

   _____

   _____

   _____

   _____

   b. How should this apply to your desire to call forth the power of God in a situation?

   _____

   _____

   _____

12. What are you told to do in Colossians 3:17?

   _____

   _____

   _____

124

Explain what you think this means.

_____

_____

_____

13. When you draw apart with Jesus, His life is nurtured within. Out of oneness with Him flows *His* power.

   a. What is a critical perspective for you to have as you experience the power of Jesus' name? See Acts 3:12-16 and 2 Corinthians 4:7.

   _____

   _____

   _____

   _____

   b. Read John 14:10, 20, and 21 and explain this outworking of Jesus through you.

   _____

   _____

   _____

   _____

14. One way to exercise the power in Jesus' name is expressed in John 14:13-14 and 16:23. What is it?

   _____

   _____

15. Think about what is on your heart today for which you would like to see Jesus' power released. What is your heart's desire for the end result in each?

_____

_____

_____

_____

_____

_____

Jesus' Lordship

16. How has Jesus' lordship been portrayed through the questions in this chapter thus far?

_____

_____

_____

_____

17. Read Philippians 2:6-11 for a summary of the Person of Jesus Christ.

    a. What do you learn about Jesus' name in verse 9?

    _____

    _____

    _____

126

b. At the name of Jesus, how will time and history climax?

_____

_____

_____

18. How does knowing of Jesus' reign help you in the following?

a. When you get discouraged

_____

_____

_____

b. In your perspective on your life and its priorities

_____

_____

_____

c. In your own relationship with the Lord

_____

_____

_____

19. Jesus is "King of kings and Lord of lords" (Revelation 19:16). What did Thomas call the risen Savior? Look up John 20:28.

_____

_____

How do you wish to express your relationship to Jesus Christ?

_____

_____

_____

_____

In the name of Jesus, Amen.

Questions for Further Discussion

Question 1: Who is Jesus according to Matthew 1:21-23, Acts 10:43, Romans 1:2-4, and 1 Peter 1:10-11? What claims did Jesus make for Himself? Read Matthew 28:18, John 5:39, 8:58, and 10:38.

Question 2: In focusing only on the truths of Jesus as your close Friend and as One who loves little children, what can happen to your concept of Him? How can this hinder all that He can be to you? Has this happened to some degree in your relationship? How can this be prevented?

Question 3: How can repeating the name of Jesus drive away fear, give you an awareness of His presence, and peace? Do this at various times, in a variety of circumstances. What do you discover? Can you give an example of a time when repeating His name has helped you?

Questions 4-6: All these gifts and promises are wrapped up in the Person of Jesus Christ. When He lives in us, we have life; and in that life, salvation and complete forgiveness (see Romans 8:1). Have you received all this? If not, or if you are unsure, simply ask Him to come and live within you. If you wish, write out your request to Him. He promises that if you ask, He will come in.

Question 8: What does Jesus say in John 14:12? What are your reactions to this? Do you desire to be God's instrument in this way? Are you afraid of this in any way? Do you fear what might happen to your faith if "nothing happens"? Is Christ's power exhibited today in observable ways? Why or why not? Give examples.

Question 9: In *Drumbeat of Love* Lloyd J. Ogilvie comments on this passage: "The only one who can use the name of Jesus is one in whom the Spirit of Jesus dwells. The exorcists wanted to exploit the power they had observed in Paul without having a relationship with the Savior he preached; they were selling a religion. . . . When people use the name of Jesus carelessly for personal gain without personal commitment to Him, they call forth not Jesus, but the forces of evil. He will not be manipulated! Jesus is not an

129

errand boy. He works miracles, not tricks of magic. And the greatest miracle is the transformation of a human heart by the power of love."[2] What are your temptations in knowing the power of Christ? (Consider His temptations in the wilderness in Luke 4:1-12.)

Question 10: How are these truths represented in Acts 4:13?

Question 11: Read the incident in Luke 7:7-10. What did the centurion recognize about Christ? Do you have such faith in the authority of Jesus? Do you want the request of a little boy's father in Mark 9:24 to be your prayer as well?

Question 12: How can this apply to your mundane tasks—or does it? How would the criterion "Can I do this in the name of Jesus" help you in what you do and say?

Question 13: How is this endorsed in Psalm 23:3 and 2 Thessalonians 1:12?

Question 14: What do you think Jesus is implying regarding your being able to use His name effectively in a request?

Question 16: What is promised in Acts 17:25 and 28? What does this say regarding your fulfillment as a person? Where do people often seek life other than in Jesus Christ? What is your greatest temptation?

For truly effective living, experiencing oneness with Jesus Christ, walking in His Spirit, and knowing His mind, what do you need to do? How will you implement this in your days? Be specific.

Question 17: What strikes you personally from this passage?

Question 18: How might knowledge of Jesus' victory help you in these situations: 1) when you feel misunderstood or persecuted in your faith; 2) your personal outreach, service, or ministry; 3) when you're filled with joy and love for the Lord; 4) other?

Notes
1. Herbert Lockyer, *All the Divine Names and Titles in the Bible* (Grand Rapids, Michigan: Zondervan Publishing House, 1975), page 174.
2. Lloyd J. Ogilvie, *Drumbeat of Love* (Waco, Texas: Word Books, 1979), page 244.